the
SPIRIT-FILLED
LIFE

ALL
THE
FULLNESS
OF
GOD

BAPTIZED | ADOPTED | TRANSFORMED | EQUIPPED | EMPOWERED | ANOINTED

Published by Bible Study Media, Inc.
www.biblestudymedia.com
www.christianlifetrilogy.com

ISBN: 978-1-942243-08-3
Printed in the United States of America.

CONTENTS

SESSIONS

APPENDICES

SMALL GROUP LEADERS

ENDORS

Charlie Holt brings us to the foot of the cross and the very heart of the Christian gospel. He invites us to ponder the death of Jesus for us and our own death to self in response to him. Powerful, compelling, transformative; a wonderful study for LENT or any other time.

The Rt. Rev. John W. Howe, Retired Bishop of the Diocese of Central Florida

The *Christian Life Trilogy* is masterfully written to tie in both an excellent small group curriculum and challenging daily devotions. This curriculum is a must for all churches desiring to have Jesus' life, death, and resurrection impact the way they go about their daily work and life. If you're a church who follows the traditional church calendar...it's a no brainer to let this excellent curriculum guide you through Lent, Easter, and Pentecost in a way you have never experienced before!

The Rev. Wes Sharp, Discipleship Priest, St. Peter's Episcopal Church, Lake Mary, FL

Many people write on topics of which they have little to no experience. Charlie Holt is different. He writes of evangelism as a result of growing a congregation. What he shares is the real deal!

The Rt. Rev. Jay Lambert, Bishop of the Diocese of Eau Claire

Fr. Charlie is a gifted teacher and his passion for the Scripture brings the Word alive for all. His enthusiasm for helping others grow in faith, his compassion for God's people and his deeply rooted relationship with Jesus make him an ideal person to create and share this transforming work.

The Ven. Kristi Alday, Archdeacon of the Diocese of Central Florida

Father Charlie Holt's *Christian Life Trilogy* offers all Christians not only a profound study of Scripture, but even more importantly, a direct and practical means of applying the eternal truths of Christ's death and resurrection to meet the challenges and frustrations of daily life.

Roni H.

4

EMENTS

In his series, Father Charlie Holt offers believing Christians new reflections on the sublime lessons of Christ's sacrifice for us, while at the same time offering means whereby we as individuals can apply the lessons of Calvary to our own lives. The series is an important opportunity to grow in faith by means of encouragement and meditation, especially as regards the self-examination that all Christians are called upon to do in our walk.

Martha Hoeber

I have attended many of Father Charlie's wonderful classes on the workings and the words of the LORD, and I believe there is no one more qualified nor one more driven through guidance of the Holy Spirit than Charlie Holt. For those of us who love the Bible, his ability to sort out complicated issues into meaningful and straightforward application is unparalleled.

Jim Grisham

I've been taught that a godly vision is born out of a recognized need in the people of God. Out of his passion for Christ, Charlie Holt has recognized a need in the people of God to grow together in community through a deeper understanding of Christ crucified, resurrected and ascended. The new small group series, *Christian Life Trilogy*, satisfies that need.

The Rev. James Sorvillo, Rector of the Church of the Ascension, Orlando, FL

The Crucified Life: Seven Words from the Cross will open your eyes to the significance and implications for your life of each and every word spoken by our Savior in His last moments on earth. What a blessing this study was for me! Taste this Spirit-led food for your Lenten experience.

Elizabeth Barber

Having already experienced *The Crucified Life: Seven Words from The Cross*, I can attest to the incredible impact of these messages from Jesus to us, as explored by Rev. Holt. The *Christian Life Trilogy* will reach into virtually every aspect of your life, ensuring that you will deepen your adoration for the Lord that loves you without end.

Laurie Mealor

ACKNOWLE

This project is offered to the glory of God for the renewal of the Church; and, with gratitude for the following people and organizations for their support and participation in this project:

Mrs. Brooke Holt
Mr. Matthew Ainsley
The Ven. Kristi Alday
The Rev. Wally Arp
The Rev. Jabriel S. Ballentine
Mr. Josh Bales
Mrs. Elizabeth Barber
Mr. Brian Bolton
Mrs. Nina Bolton
Ms. Helen Bostick
Mr. Robert Boarders
The Rev. Sarah Bronos
Mr. F. Scott Brown
Mrs. Candy Brown
Miss Lizzy Sult Case
The Rev. Sonia Sullivan Clifton
Mr. Dalas Davis
Mr. Samuel Dunaway

DGEMENTS

Mrs. Jenna Dunaway
Mr. John Gullett
Mrs. Martha Hoeber
The Rev. Canon Justin Holcomb
Mrs. Colette Ivanov
Ms. Kathy Krasnoff
Mrs. Laurie Mealor
Ms. Virginia Mooney
Mr. James Nedved
The Rev. Canon Tim Nunez
Mrs. Ada O'Neil
The Rev. Andrew Petiprin
Mr. Gordon Sims
The Rev. Jim Sorvillo
Mrs. Heather Startup
Mr. Joe Thoma
Mr. Jarda Tusek
Mrs. Sarah Tusek

Mr. David Wellday
Mr. Todd Wilson
Mrs. Sharon Wilson
Mr. Lemar Williams
Mrs. Karen Williams
Mrs. Susie Millonig
The Rev. Dane Wren
The Very Rev. Anthony Clark
St. Peter's Episcopal Church in Lake Mary, FL
The Cathedral Church of St. Luke, Orlando, FL
Allen White & Lifetogether Ministries, Inc.

FORE

WORD

Spirit-Filled Life

The Christian life is a series of journeys. Some journeys are taken entirely alone, guided only by the unseen presence of Christ working in our hearts and guiding our circumstances. Other journeys are taken with others—sometimes serendipitously and sometimes intentionally. This series invites us into a short-term but intentional journey with others. And this journey is an adventure well worth taking.

By embarking on this journey, you are committing to lively conversations, Bible study, and prayer. These commitments are not haphazard; they are purposeful, for Christians believe that it is through these activities that we often discover the presence of the Holy Spirit. That is not to say that these activities are easy. In fact, they can (and should be) deeply challenging. But if we enter into them prayerfully and intentionally, they can lead us into deep and positive personal change. The miracle is that God uses these activities to reveal His Spirit and help us, amazingly, to see where and how His Spirit is at work in us.

Fr. Charlie Holt invites us on this journey as a gentle and thoughtful guide. He is aware of the potential hazards of small group activity as well as its joys, and offers both leaders and participants clear boundaries and open-ended possibilities. I would invite you to join him and others in this adventure!

- **The Rt. Rev. Gregory O. Brewer**
Bishop of the Episcopal Diocese of Central Florida

WELC

Welcome to *The Spirit-Filled Life*. Over the next six weeks, you will experience the joy of life in community as you come together to listen, discuss, reflect, and grow together in your lives of faith.

When God created the world, He pronounced His creation "good," with one exception: man's being alone. Being alone was "not good," said God. We as human beings need each other. Jesus called 12 disciples to come alongside Him during His earthly ministry. We are designed for community, to live our lives alongside and in companionship with others. In the context of community, we connect with one another and with God in life-changing ways.

This unique small group curriculum will give you the opportunity to hear in-depth Biblical teaching and then openly discuss that teaching in your group, wrestling together with God's Word and providing mutual support as you allow your life to be transformed by what you discover. The curriculum is designed to connect your weekly small group study with your individual daily times with God as well as what you hear in church each week.

This curriculum is centered on a DVD teaching series focused on the creative and life-giving work of the Holy Spirit in our lives. There are **six unique teaching sessions,** one for each lesson. In your small group, you will watch the DVD teaching together, then dig deeper through the Scriptures and questions provided. Each Sunday, you will discover how the Scriptures and homilies you experience in church are related to the small group teaching.

At the end of each session in this study guide, you'll be referred to the corresponding Daily Devotions in *The Spirit-Filled Life* book for the upcoming week. These devotions will help you **further explore what**

COME

the weekly teaching means in your life. There's also a Scripture verse that we hope you will commit to memory as well as a place to record your own personal reflections.

We trust that *The Spirit-Filled Life* curriculum will provide a positive introduction to small group community for those who are new, as well as a rich and rewarding experience to those who are veterans of small groups.

In all of this, our prayer is that you would experience God and the truths of the Scriptures in a powerful new way as you take part in this small group study.

INTROD

WELCOME TO *the* SPIRIT-FILLED LIFE.

The Christian Life is a movement from Crucified to Resurrected to Spirit-Filled! Congratulations on making this journey with Jesus Christ.

UCTION

With the outpouring of the Holy Spirit on the day of Pentecost, we entered into the final phase of God's plan of redemption and salvation for the world. As we explored in *The Resurrected Life* study, forty days after Jesus rose from the dead he ascended into the heavenly realms and took the throne of heaven at the right hand of God the Father (Acts 1:1-10). Fifty days after the resurrection, Jesus poured out the promised Holy Spirit on the church gathered in Jerusalem and inaugurated, with all authority and power, the New Covenant between God and humanity (Acts 2:1-41).

In the letter to the church of Ephesus, the Apostle Paul outlines the grand plan of God in Jesus Christ to redeem and restore the cosmos. Paul describes this plan as one to be put into effect "when the times reach their fulfillment." The plan is pretty straightforward—*to bring unity to all things in heaven and on earth under Christ* (Ephesians 1:10).

The two agents actively bringing about Christ's rule on earth as *it is in heaven* are the Holy Spirit **and us!** When you and I believed in Jesus Christ as Lord and Savior of the world, we became beneficiaries and agents of the plan of redemption. **You** are an appointed ambassador, entrusted with the *"word of truth, the gospel of your salvation"* (Ephesians 1:13, ESV). Here is the profound promise given to those who believe:

When you believed, you were marked in him with a seal, the promised Holy Spirit, who is a deposit guaranteeing our inheritance until the redemption of those who are God's possession—to the praise of his glory (Ephesians 1:13-14).

During the next six sessions of *The Spirit-Filled Life* study, you will explore how God's will for you is to baptize, adopt, transform, equip, empower, and anoint you by, with, in and through the Holy Spirit. The six sessions are: ·

- Baptized: The Outpouring of the Spirit
- Adopted: The Calling of the Spirit
- Transformed: The Fruit of the Spirit
- Equipped: The Gifts of the Spirit
- Empowered: The Work of the Spirit
- Anointed: The Mission of the Spirit

I pray that as you embark on this next study in the *Christian Life Trilogy*, in community with others, God will fill you with all the fullness of His Holy Spirit. My prayer for you is joined with that of the Apostle Paul for the church:

For this reason, because I have heard of your faith in the Lord Jesus and your love toward all the saints, I do not cease to give thanks for you, remembering you in my prayers, that the God of our Lord Jesus Christ, the Father of glory, may give you the Spirit of wisdom and of revelation in the knowledge of him, having the eyes of your hearts enlightened, that you may know what is the hope to which he has called you, what are the riches of his glorious inheritance in the saints, and what is the immeasurable greatness of his power toward us who believe, according to the working of his great might that he worked in Christ when he raised him from the dead and seated him at his right hand in the heavenly places, far above all rule and authority and power and dominion, and above every name that is named, not only in this age but also in the one to come. And he put all things under his feet and gave him as head over all things to the church, which is his body, the fullness of him who fills all in all.

--Ephesians 1:15-22, ESV

Charlie †

USING *this* WORKBOOK

Tools to Help You Have a Great Small Group Experience

1 Notice the Table of Contents is divided into three sections: (1) Sessions; (2) Appendices; and (3) Small Group Leaders. Familiarize yourself with the Appendices. Some of them will be used in the sessions themselves.

2 If you are facilitating/leading or co-leading a small group, the section Small Group Leaders will offer you some hard-learned insights from the experiences of others that will encourage you and help you avoid common obstacles to effective small group leadership.

3 Use this workbook as a guide, not a straightjacket. If the group responds to the lesson in an unexpected but honest way, go with that. If you think of a better question than the next one in the lesson, ask it. Take to heart the insights included in the Frequently Asked Questions pages and the Small Group Leaders section.

4 You may find that you can't get through all the questions in a given lesson in the time you have. Look for the questions marked with an asterisk, and use those first if you're short on time.

5 Enjoy your small group experience.

6 Pray before each session—for your group members, for your time together, for wisdom and insight.

7 Read the Outline for Each Session on the next pages so that you understand how the sessions will flow.

OUTLINE *of* EACH SESSION

A typical group session for The Spirit-Filled Life study will include the following sections:

WEEKLY MEMORY VERSES. Each session opens with a Memory Verse that emphasizes an important truth from the session. This is an optional exercise, but we believe that memorizing Scripture can be a vital part of filling our minds with God's truth for our lives. We encourage you to give this important habit a try. The verses for our seven sessions are also listed in the appendix.

SHARE YOUR STORY. The foundation for spiritual growth is an intimate connection with God and His family. You build that connection in part by sharing your story with a few people who really know you and who earn your trust. This section includes some simple questions to get you talking—letting you share as much or as little of your story as you feel comfortable doing. Each session typically offers you two options. You can get to know your whole group by using the icebreaker question(s), or you may also desire to check in with one or two group members, in between weekly sessions, for a deeper connection and encouragement in your spiritual journey.

HEAR GOD'S STORY. In this section, you'll read the Biblical passages and listen to teaching—in order to better understand God's story of creation and redemption and discover how your story connects to the larger story of the Bible. When the study directs you, you'll turn on the DVD and watch a short

teaching segment. You'll then have an opportunity to read a passage of Scripture and discuss both the teaching and the text. You'll be gleaning new insights from God's Word, and then discussing how you should live in light of these truths. We want to help you apply the insights from Scripture practically and creatively, from your heart as well as your head. At the end of the day, allowing the timeless truths from God's Word to transform our lives in Christ should be your greatest aim.

STUDY NOTES. This brief section provides additional commentary, background or insights into the passage you'll study in the *Hear God's Story* section.

CREATE A NEW STORY. God wants you to be a part of His Kingdom—to weave your story into His. That will mean change. It will require you to go His way rather than your own. This won't happen overnight, but it should happen steadily. By making small, simple choices, we can begin to change our direction. This is where the Bible's instruction to be "doers of the Word, not just hearers" (James 1:22) comes into play. Many people skip over this aspect of the Christian life because it can be frightening, difficult, relationally awkward or simply too much work for our busy schedules. But Jesus wanted all of His disciples to know Him personally, carry out His commands, and help outsiders connect with Him. This doesn't necessarily mean preaching on street corners. It could mean welcoming newcomers, hosting a short-term group in your home, or walking through this study with a friend. In this study, you'll have an opportunity to go beyond Bible study to biblical living. This section will also have a question or two that will challenge you to live out your faith by serving others, sharing your faith, and worshiping God.

FOR ADDITIONAL STUDY. If you have time and want to dig deeper into more Bible passages about the topic at hand, we've provided additional passages and questions. Your group may choose to read and prepare ahead of each meeting in order to cover more biblical material. If you prefer not to do study homework, this section will provide you with plenty to discuss within the group. These options allow individuals or the whole group to expand their study while still accommodating those who can't do homework or are new to your group. You can discuss this in your group or just study it on your own, whatever your group prefers.

DAILY DEVOTIONS. Each week under the heading Daily Devotions, we refer you to the Daily Devotions found in *The Spirit-Filled Life* companion book. There is much more to learn and consider in the book *The Spirit-Filled Life*, material that is not covered in the small group material. We encourage you to set aside a time each day for these devotions. The practice will give you a chance to slow down, delve more deeply into the weekly teaching and pray through it. Use this time to seek God on your own throughout the week. Try not to rush; take the time to truly ponder God's Word and listen for His direction.

ALL THE FULLNESS OF GOD

BAPTIZED

The Outpouring of the Spirit

And hope does not put us to shame, because God's love has been poured out into our hearts through the Holy Spirit, who has been given to us.

ROMANS 5:5

This study, *The Spirit-Filled Life*, invites us to examine and better understand the transformative role of the Holy Spirit in our lives. After receiving the sacrament of baptism, we are welcomed into a life of faith marked by the presence and gifts of the Holy Spirit.

Notice in the verse from Romans, above, that God's love is *poured out* through the Holy Spirit; it is not given to us in tiny drops or by the spoonful. God lavishly floods our hearts; He wants us to be filled to brimming with His love.

In this study, we will explore what it means to walk "in the Spirit" and to see more clearly the life-giving and creative work of the Holy Spirit in our hearts and minds.

THIS WEEK, WE'LL ASK:

- Who is the Holy Spirit?
- In what ways is the Spirit a sign of God's keeping His promises?
- How might we best respond to this generous gift?

SHARE *your* STORY

Each of us has a story. The events of our life—good, bad, wonderful or challenging—have shaped who we are. God knows your story, and He intends to redeem it—to use every struggle and every joy to ultimately bring you to Himself. When we share our stories with others, we give them the opportunity to see God at work.

When we share our stories, we realize we are not alone—that we have common experiences and thoughts, and that others can understand what we are going through. Your story can encourage someone else, and telling it can be a path to freedom for you, and for those with whom you share it.

Open your group with prayer. This should be a brief, simple prayer in which you invite God to guide you as you meet. You can pray for specific requests at the end of the meeting, or stop momentarily to pray if a particular situation comes up during your discussion.

If you prefer, you could use a collect from the *Book of Common Prayer* to begin your time together, such as:

O God, who dost manifest in thy servants the signs of thy presence: Send forth upon us the Spirit of love, that in companionship with one another thine abounding grace may increase among us; through Jesus Christ our Lord. Amen. (BCP, p. 71.)

As you begin, pass around a copy of the *Small Group Roster* on page 130, a sheet of paper, or have one member pass around their Study Guide, opened to the *Small Group Roster*. Have everyone introduce themselves and write down their contact information. Ask someone to make copies or type up a list with everyone's information and email it to the group during the week.

Then, begin your time together by using the following questions and activities to get people talking.

READ MATTHEW 3:11

I baptize you with water for repentance. But after me comes one who is more powerful than I, whose sandals I am not worthy to carry. He will baptize you with the Holy Spirit and fire.

1. What brought you here? What do you hope to get out of this group?

2. What images come to mind when you think of the Holy Spirit? A dove? Wind? Fire? Water?

3. Which member of the Trinity do you feel most connected to: the Father, Son, or Holy Spirit? Why do you think that is? Have you always felt that way?

4. How would you describe your relationship with the third person of the Trinity—God the Holy Spirit?

5. Whether your group is new or ongoing, it's always important to reflect on and review your values together. On page 124 is a *Small Group Agreement* with the values we've found most useful in sustaining healthy, balanced groups. We recommend that you choose one or two values—ones you haven't previously focused on or have room to grow in—to emphasize during this study. Choose ones that will take your group to the next stage of intimacy and spiritual health.

- If your group is new, welcome newcomers. Introduce everyone— you may even want to have nametags for your first meeting.

- We recommend that you rotate host homes on a regular basis and let the hosts lead the meeting. Studies show that healthy groups rotate leadership. This helps to develop every member's ability to shepherd a few people in a safe environment. Even Jesus gave others the opportunity to serve alongside Him (Mark 6:30–44). Look at the FAQs in the Appendix "Additional Information" about hosting or leading the group.

- The *Small Group Calendar* on page 126 is a tool for planning who will host and lead each meeting. Take a few minutes to plan hosts and leaders for your remaining meetings. Don't skip this important step! It will revolutionize your group.

SPIRIT-FILLED

WATCH *now*

DVD SESSION ONE

Watch the DVD for this session now. Use the Notes space to record your thoughts, questions, and ponderings as you watch the video and discuss the Bible passage.

After watching the video, have someone read the discussion questions in the *Hear God's Story* section and direct the discussion among the group. As you go through each of the subsequent sections of this study, ask someone else to read the next question and rotate who directs the discussion.

HEAR *God's* STORY

READ ACTS 2:38

Peter replied, "Repent and be baptized, every one of you, in the name of Jesus Christ for the forgiveness of your sins. And you will receive the gift of the Holy Spirit.

God uses stories to guide us. When we read the true stories of Scripture, we learn what God is like and we see His plan unfolding. And we learn principles for our own lives. How can we become a part of God's story? By aligning our stories with His. By not just understanding what it means to follow Him, but actually doing it—changing our attitudes and actions to live as He would live. Use the following questions to guide your discussion of the teaching and stories you just heard, as well as the Bible passage below. You may want to use the study notes on page 31 to guide your reading and discussion.

1. In the DVD, Fr. Charlie describes the Holy Spirit as "the creative and life-giving force of God." In what times of life have you felt the presence of the Holy Spirit? For example, when you create or experience a work of art? When you are inspired to serve others? When you witness another person's baptism? Give an example of a time when you have sensed the presence of the Holy Spirit.

2. Do you remember your own baptism or that of someone you love (a friend, your child, others)? Talk about what a person may see, hear, and feel when he or she is baptized or while witnessing a baptism. Think through all of the senses and how we experience baptism.

3. At baptism, we recite the Baptismal Covenant. The covenant ends with the questions below. Take a moment to read and reflect on the promises made in baptism:

-    Will you proclaim by word and example the Good News of God in Christ?

-    Will you seek and serve Christ in all persons, loving your neighbor as yourself?

-    Will you strive for justice and peace among all people, and respect the dignity of every human being?

We answer these questions, "I will, with God's help."

Talk about a time when you have had the opportunity to proclaim the Good News, love your neighbor, or strive for justice and peace. How did the Holy Spirit of God *help* you in fulfillment of those promises?

4. In the teaching, Fr. Charlie described baptism as a "sacrament," or an outward and visible sign of an inward and spiritual grace. What does the sacrament of baptism mean to you? When someone is baptized, how is she or he affected spiritually?

STUDY

NOTES

GRACE. Fr. Charlie notes that, in baptism, we enter into the repentance, forgiveness, and filling of the Spirit. Baptism is the starting point of the Christian life. We experience a new birth and a new life in Christ. The outward and visible sign of the waters of baptism signify and point to the inward and spiritual grace of rebirth and new life for those reborn in the Holy Spirit. This new life is not dependent upon our good works or our efforts to live a better life, but rather, new life is a gift from God.

CHRIST'S BAPTISM. John the Baptist asked Jesus why He needed to be baptized when He was sinless. Although we must repent and be baptized, Christ had no sin to confess and did not need redemption because He was perfect. Jesus' baptism not only fulfilled all righteousness on our behalf, but also inaugurated His kingdom ministry as the Son of God. After His baptism by water, the Holy Spirit "descended like a dove" and filled Him. Jesus' baptism anticipates his death on the cross and resurrection with power.

OUR BAPTISM. Likewise, after we repent and are baptized into the family of God, God's Holy Spirit will come upon us and inaugurate our entrance into Christ's Kingdom. Water baptism signifies our spiritual baptism into Christ's death, burial, and resurrection.

CREATE *a* NEW STORY

God wants you to be a part of His Kingdom—to weave your story into His. That will mean change, going His way rather than your own. This won't happen overnight, but it should happen steadily. By starting with small, simple choices, we begin to change our direction. The Holy Spirit helps us along the way—giving us gifts to serve the body, offering us insights into Scripture, and challenging us to love not only those around us but those far from God.

In this section, talk about how you will apply the wisdom you've learned from the teaching and Bible study. Then think about practical steps you can take in the coming week to live out what you've learned.

1. In the Old Testament, God promises that when His new covenant comes, He will put His law "into the people's hearts." In what ways do you feel that God's law is "written on" your heart? Talk about a time when your conscience was troubled and the Holy Spirit might have encouraged you to make different choices or nudged you toward a higher calling?

2. Talk about a time when you felt that someone you met was filled with the Holy Spirit. What was this person like? What were his or her priorities? In what ways could this person serve as a model to you as you move through the week?

3. Identify a situation this week that you can handle differently than you have in the past, keeping in mind that you have received the gift of the Holy Spirit.

4. To close your time together, spend some time worshiping God— praying, singing, reading Scripture. Here are some ideas:

- Have someone use their musical gifts to lead the group in a worship song. Try singing a cappella, using a worship CD, or have someone accompany your singing with a musical instrument.

- Choose a psalm or other favorite verse and read it aloud together. Make it a time of praise and worship, as the words remind you of all God has done for you.

- Ask "How can we pray for you this week?" Invite everyone to share, but don't force the issue. Be sure to write prayer requests on your *Prayer and Praise Report* on page 128.

- Close your meeting with prayer. You might want to pray, as Fr. Charlie suggests, a simple prayer to welcome the Holy Spirit such as this one: *Lord, fill me with your Holy Spirit.*

for ADDITIONAL STUDY

If you feel God nudging you to go deeper, take some time between now and our next meeting to dig into His Word. Explore the Bible passages related to this session's theme on your own, jotting your reflections in a journal or in this study guide. A great way to gain insight on a passage is to read it in several different translations. You may want to use a Bible app or website to compare translations.

READ MATTHEW 3:8

Produce fruit in keeping with repentance.

John the Baptist instructs the people to repent and to "produce fruit." In upcoming weeks of this study, we will more closely consider the fruit and gifts of the Holy Spirit. This week, try to be intentional about observing your own actions and those of the people around you. Ask yourself how the presence of the Holy Spirit is working through you this week. Consider how others are bearing fruit, given the Spirit's presence in them.

READ MATTHEW 3:16-17

As soon as Jesus was baptized, he went up out of the water. At that moment heaven was opened, and he saw the Spirit of God descending like a dove and alighting on him. And a voice from heaven said, "This is my Son, whom I love; with him I am well pleased."

Picture the scene, described above in the verses from Matthew. What would it have been like to be John the Baptist, who had just—somewhat reluctantly—baptized Christ? What would it feel like to be on the shores of the river Jordan and to see the Spirit "descending like a dove" and to have heard God's voice speak words of love for Jesus?

Take a few minutes to write an imagined journal entry by someone who had witnessed these things. Perhaps, imagining that you had witnessed Jesus' baptism, you will feel a new motivation to ask in response: "What, then, shall I do?"

extra notes

....

....

....

....

....

....

....

....

....

....

....

....

....

....

....

....

DAILY

DEVOTIONS

Remember to set aside time each day to read the Daily Devotion found in *The Spirit-Filled Life* companion book. These devotions will help you go deeper into this week's teaching. Listen to what God wants to say to you through His Word, and respond to Him as you meditate on the truths of Scripture.

ADOPTED

The Calling of the Spirit

He predestined us for adoption to sonship through Jesus Christ, in accordance with his pleasure and will.

EPHESIANS 1:5

In his teaching this week, Fr. Charlie compares the pain and challenges children experience as they grow and mature into adults with the suffering and struggle of becoming free from our sinful natures and becoming more like Christ—even after receiving His forgiveness and being filled by the Spirit.

We are God's cherished, adopted children. However, in order to fully enjoy the love of God and the life He offers, we must break the bonds that tie us to old, harmful patterns of thinking and behavior.

Fortunately, we are promised that there is "no condemnation in Christ," so as we seek freedom from our sinful tendencies, we can do so with the assurance that we are in a real relationship with a loving God—from which nothing on earth or heaven can separate us!

Together this week, we'll explore what this relationship looks and feels like.

SHARE *your* STORY

As we said last week, when we tell our stories, sharing them with others, we give others the opportunity to see God at work. Your story is being shaped, even in this moment, by being a part of this group. In fact, few things can shape us more than community.

When we share our stories, we can encourage someone else, and learn. We can experience the presence of God as He helps us be brave enough to reveal our thoughts and feelings.

Open your group with prayer. This should be a brief, simple prayer in which you invite God to guide you as you meet and to give you insight and wisdom. You can pray for specific requests at the end of the meeting, or stop momentarily to pray if a particular situation comes up during your discussion.

If you prefer, you could use this prayer from the *Book of Common Prayer* (BCP, p. 125):

O God, you manifest in your servants the signs of your presence: Send forth upon us the Spirit of love, that in companionship with one another your abounding grace may increase among us; through Jesus Christ our Lord. Amen.

Then, begin your time together by using the following questions and activities to generate discussion in your group.

1. How would you define "human nature"? Do you see "sinful nature" as different from "human nature"? Talk about how you understand the meaning of these two phrases.

2. Have you ever witnessed someone who seemed "at war" with himself or herself? Did he or she repeatedly engage in regretful or destructive behavior and then bear the burden of feeling guilty or suffer other consequences? Or, what behavior patterns did you observe? When have you felt "at war" with yourself?

extra NOTES

~~08-16~~ - 5-22-16

Our cry out to God during
our struggles, is assurance
we are true children of God.

WATCH *now*

DVD SESSION TWO

Watch the DVD for this session now. Use the Notes space to record your thoughts, questions, and ponderings as you watch the video and discuss the Bible passage.

HEAR *God's* STORY

READ ROMANS 8:26-27

In the same way, the Spirit helps us in our weakness. We do not know what we ought to pray for, but the Spirit himself intercedes for us through wordless groans. And he who searches our hearts knows the mind of the Spirit, because the Spirit intercedes for God's people in accordance with the will of God.

How can we become a part of God's story? By aligning our stories with His. By understanding what it means to follow Him. Use the following questions to guide your discussion of the teaching and stories you just experienced, and the Bible passage on this page.

1. What's your experience of adoption? Do you have family members or friends who were adopted or who adopted children? Describe these children's homecomings and transitions into their new family. In what ways can you draw comparisons between your spiritual adoption into God's family and these human adoptions?

2. Fr. Charlie said that it took forty years for the children of Israel to break their slave mentality after being imprisoned in Egypt before they could enter the Promised Land. Talk about a time when you felt held captive by old patterns of thinking. What did it take to free you?

3. Do you ever wonder—perhaps especially at times when you find yourself unable to get distance from a harmful or sinful pattern in your own life—if you really are a child of God? How do you pray when you have feelings of isolation or doubt? In what ways have you been comforted in such times?

extra notes

....
....
....
....
....
....
....
....
....
....
....
....
....
....
....
....
....
....
....

STUDY

NOTES

YOU WERE A SLAVE. The slave mentality is hard to break. Without Jesus and the Holy Spirit, we are in bondage under the Law of God and the Law of Sin. Jesus' death on the cross frees us from condemnation due to breaking the Law of God. The Holy Spirit frees us from the chains of the Law of Sin.

YOU ARE GOD'S CHILD. In his teaching, Fr. Charlie encourages us to reflect on the fact that we are God's adopted sons and daughters. He tells the story of his daughter calling him "Abba" instead of "Daddy" when she was very young. Have you ever cried out to God the Father in such a vulnerable, trusting way, as if you were shouting, "Daddy!"? Is this a new way for you to see your relationship with God?

CREATE *a* NEW STORY

In this section, talk about how you will apply the wisdom you've learned from the teaching and Bible study. Then think about practical steps you can take in the coming week to live out what you've learned.

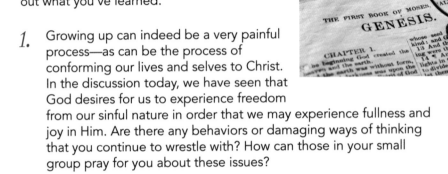

1. Growing up can indeed be a very painful process—as can be the process of conforming our lives and selves to Christ. In the discussion today, we have seen that God desires for us to experience freedom from our sinful nature in order that we may experience fullness and joy in Him. Are there any behaviors or damaging ways of thinking that you continue to wrestle with? How can those in your small group pray for you about these issues?

2. Fr. Charlie reminds us in this week's teaching that God loves us, chose us, calls us, has justified us, and will complete the work He began in us. Talk about some of the ways you have seen God heal you from old wounds, freeing you up to enjoy Him more.

3. How does knowing you are loved, chosen, called, and justified impact the way that you treat other people?

4. Spend some time praying about those you know who might respond to a simple invitation: to come to a church service, to join your small group, or even just to have coffee and talk about spiritual matters. Ask the Holy Spirit to bring to mind people you can pray for.

5. Take a look at the *Circles of Life* diagram below and write the names of two or three friends or acquaintances who haven't heard about the abundant new life Christ offers or who might not yet have a sense that there is nothing that can separate them from God's love. Commit to praying for God's guidance and an opportunity to share with each of them. Share your lists with the group so that you can all be praying for the people you've identified.

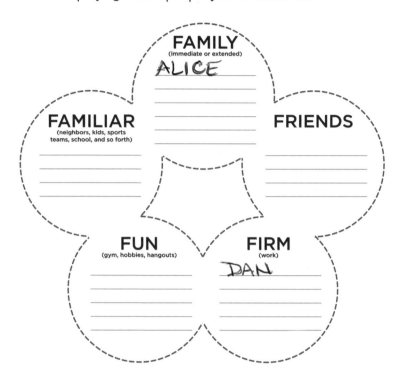

6. Developing our ability to serve according to the leading of the Holy Spirit takes time and persistence in getting to know our Lord. So the first step toward serving others is, paradoxically, spending time alone with God: praying, studying, and reflecting on God's Word. Here are some simple ways to connect with God. Tell the group which one you plan to try this week, and then talk about your progress and challenges when you meet next time.

- **Prayer.** Commit to personal prayer and daily connection with God. You may find it helpful to write your prayers in a journal.

- **Daily Devotions.** The Daily Devotions provided in *The Spirit-Filled Life* companion book offer an opportunity to read a short Bible passage each day during the course of this study. In our hurry-up world, we often move too quickly through everything—even reading God's Word! Slow down. Don't just skim, but take time to read carefully and reflect on the passage. Write down your insights into what you read each day. Copy a portion of Scripture on a card and tape it somewhere in your line of sight, such as your car's dashboard or the bathroom mirror. Or text it to yourself! Think about it when you sit at red lights, or while you're eating a meal. Reflect on what God is saying to you through these words. On the seventh day, summarize what God has shown you throughout the week.

7. This week, how will you interact with the Bible? Can you commit to spending time in daily prayer or study of God's Word? Tell the group how you plan to follow Jesus this week, and then, at your next meeting, talk about your progress and challenges.

8. To close your time together, spend some time worshiping God together—praying, singing, reading Scripture. Try one of these ideas:

- Have someone use their musical gifts to lead the group in a worship song. Try singing a cappella, using a worship CD, or have someone accompany your singing with a musical instrument.

- Choose a psalm or other favorite verse and read it aloud together. Make it a time of praise and worship, as the words remind you of all God has done for you.

- Ask "How can we pray for you this week?" Invite everyone to share, but don't force the issue. Be sure to write prayer requests on your *Prayer and Praise Report* on page 128.

- Close your meeting with prayer.

for ADDITIONAL STUDY

If you feel God nudging you to go deeper, take some time between now and our next meeting to dig into His Word. Explore the Bible passages below on your own, jotting your reflections in a journal or in this study guide. Want to go deeper? Select a few verses and try paraphrasing them: writing them in your own words. If you like, share them with the group the next time you meet.

READ ROMANS 8:38-39

For I am convinced that neither death nor life, neither angels nor demons, neither the present nor the future, nor any powers, neither height nor depth, nor anything else in all creation, will be able to separate us from the love of God that is in Christ Jesus our Lord.

Have you ever felt like something you've said, done, or thought has separated you from God's love? Read St. Paul's bold proclamation above—nothing in "all creation" can separate us from Christ's love! Claim that promise today, and as you seek to deepen spiritually, rest in that love.

READ JOHN 14:26

But the Advocate, the Holy Spirit, whom the Father will send in my name, will teach you all things and will remind you of everything I have said to you.

The Holy Spirit has many names including Advocate, Guide, Comforter, Counselor, Revealer, Teacher, and Witness. We're told that the Spirit is also Intercessor and prays for us with longing. The Spirit reminds us, inspires us, and convicts us. Which one of these titles, functions, or names describes the role you would like the Spirit to have in your own life this week?

extra notes

DAILY

DEVOTIONS

Use the Daily Devotions in *The Spirit-Filled Life* companion book to further explore this week's topic. Read the devotional reflection each day and take time to think through the questions at the end. Ask God to speak to you through His Word and to transform your life by His love and mercy.

TRANS FORMED

The Fruit of the Spirit

Do not conform to the pattern of this world, but be transformed by the renewing of your mind. Then you will be able to test and approve what God's will is—his good, pleasing and perfect will.

ROMANS 12:2

In this week's study, we will delve into the reality of the Holy Spirit's transformative work in us. The Spirit wants to change us, from the inside out. Although God created us to mirror His glory, our sin obscures His reflection. We are oriented toward other things—the trappings of our culture and desires that distract us from spiritual matters.

We are in need of transformation.

The good news is that the Holy Spirit can reverse the effects of the fall, giving us the opportunity to realign our lives with Christ. And, as Fr. Charlie says, the best way we can undergo this transformative work is in community.

This week, we will look at how our sinful nature manifests itself and find comfort and hope in God's renewing work in our hearts and minds.

SHARE *your* STORY

Open your group with prayer. This should be a brief, simple prayer in which you invite God to be with you as you meet. You can pray for specific requests at the end of the meeting, or stop momentarily to pray if a particular situation comes up during your discussion.

You could also pray this collect from the *Book of Common Prayer* (BCP, p. 124)

O God and Father of all, whom the whole heavens adore: Let the whole earth also worship you, all nations obey you, all tongues confess and bless you, and men and women everywhere love you and serve you in peace; through Jesus Christ our Lord. Amen.

Telling our personal stories builds deeper connections among group members. Begin your time together by using the following questions and activities to get people talking.

1. In what ways do you see "peer pressure" or "keeping up with the Joneses" at play in your home, neighborhood, or in the wider community?

2. If you are a parent, how do you talk with your children about peer pressure?

3. When have you felt pressure to conform, even when your own convictions and thoughts were at odds with these external demands?

extra NOTES

WATCH *now*

DVD SESSION THREE

Watch the DVD for this session now. Use the Notes space to record your thoughts, questions, and ponderings as you watch the video and discuss the Bible passage.

HEAR *God's* STORY

READ GALATIANS 5:22-23

But the fruit of the Spirit is love, joy, peace, forbearance, kindness, goodness, faithfulness, gentleness, and self-control. Against such things there is no law.

Use the following questions to guide your discussion of the teaching you just experienced on the DVD and the Bible passage on this page.

1. Look around at the members in your small group. Name a fruit of the Spirit that you observe in each member. Does one of you model gentleness? Kindness? Joy? Encourage one another by pointing out the ways you see the Holy Spirit at work in each other's lives.

2. Fr. Charlie notes that God "rubs off our rough edges" when we are living in community and especially when we spend time in the company of fellow believers. Think of an instance when working to resolve a conflict (at home, at church) has helped you mature spiritually or more fully manifest a fruit of the Spirit.

3. What's your "favorite" fruit of the Spirit? What is the most rare "fruit" in many of the people you know? Most common?

extra notes

STUDY

NOTES

LIVING SACRIFICES. Fr. Charlie noted that this phrase, used by St. Paul in Romans (Romans 12:1), seems contradictory, even an oxymoron. What could it mean when St. Paul exhorts us to be "living sacrifices" for Christ? A sacrifice, according to one of the definitions in the dictionary, is "a thing surrendered or devoted." We are told, then, to be surrendered to God's will and devoted to Christ.

WORKS OF THE FLESH. Fr. Charlie listed the manifestations of our old, sinful nature including jealousy, divisiveness, and immorality. Christians are called to have none of the works of the flesh.

FRUIT OF THE SPIRIT. When we die to our old self and live for Christ, different traits will make themselves known in us, including love, joy, peace, and patience—and all the other fruit of the Spirit. These character attributes reveal the inward transformation of the Holy Spirit. All Christians are called to bear all the fruit of the Spirit.

CREATE *a* NEW STORY

God wants you to be a part of His Kingdom— to weave your story into His. That will mean change. It will require you to go His way rather than your own. This won't happen overnight, but it should happen steadily. By making small, simple choices, we can begin to change our direction. The Holy Spirit helps us along the way by giving us gifts to serve the body, offering us insights into Scripture, and challenging us to love not only those around us but those far from God.

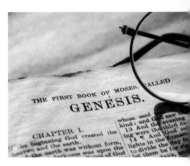

In this section, talk about how you will apply the wisdom you've learned in this session.

1. In the teaching, Fr. Charlie says that we are more likely to give in to our sinful desires when we isolate ourselves from others—when there's no one to challenge us or inspire us to make better choices. What circumstances or situations tempt you to avoid or even hide from those who might confront you? When have you sought out someone to keep you accountable?

2. This week we were reminded that we were created to worship God and to reflect Him in the world around us. In what ways is your life a mirror that reflects God's grace and/or manifests the fruit of the Spirit? How could you more clearly be a sign of God's presence to those around you this week?

3. While we are, as Fr. Charlie noted, meant to manifest *all* of the fruit of the spirit (love, joy, peace, patience, kindness...), we should have *none* of the "works of the flesh" in our life (jealousy, idolatry, fits of anger, sexual immorality...). Were there any sins or "manifestations of the flesh" that you felt convicted of when Fr. Charlie read that list? If so, bring them to Christ, ask for forgiveness, and let the Spirit fill you.

4. Spend some time praying about those you know who might respond to a simple invitation: to come to a church service, to join your small group, or even to just have coffee and talk about spiritual matters. Ask the Holy Spirit to bring to mind people you can pray for.

5. What specific steps will you take this week to cultivate your personal relationship with God? If you've focused on prayer in past weeks, maybe you'll want to direct your attention to Scripture this week. If you've been reading God's Word consistently, perhaps you'll want to take it deeper and try memorizing a verse. Tell the group which one you plan to try this week, and then, at your next meeting, talk about your progress and challenges.

6. In the last session we asked you to write some names in the *Circles of Life* diagram. Who did you identify as the people in your life who need to meet Jesus? Go back to the *Circles of Life* diagram on page 49 to help you think of the various people you come in contact with on a regular basis, people who need to know Jesus more deeply. Consider the following ideas for action and make a plan to follow through on one of them this week.

- This is a wonderful time to welcome a few friends into your group. Which of the people you listed could you invite? It's possible that you may need to help your friend overcome obstacles to coming to a place where he or she can encounter Jesus. Does your friend need a ride to the group? Help with childcare?

- Consider inviting a friend to attend a weekend service with you and possibly plan to enjoy a meal together afterward. This can be a great opportunity to talk with someone about your faith in Jesus.

- Is there someone whom you wouldn't invite to your group but who still needs connection? Would you be willing to have lunch or coffee with that person, catch up on life, and share something you've learned from this study? Jesus doesn't call all of us to lead small groups, but He does call every disciple to spiritually multiply his or her life over time.

- Groups that connect outside of the regular meeting time build stronger bonds and feel a greater sense of purpose. Why not plan a social outing with group members? As a group, brainstorm about ways that you could do something fun together—enjoy a meal or a night out together?

7. To close your time together, spend some time worshiping God— praying, singing, or reading Scripture—as you've done in previous weeks.

- Close your meeting with prayer. Be sure to write prayer requests on your *Prayer and Praise Report* on page 128.

extra NOTES

for ADDITIONAL STUDY

Take some time between now and our next meeting to dig into God's Word. Explore the Bible passages related to this session's theme on your own, jotting your reflections in a journal or in this study guide. You may even want to use a Bible website or app to look up commentary on these passages. If you like, share what you learn with the group the next time you meet.

READ GALATIANS 5:24-25

Those who belong to Christ Jesus have crucified the flesh with its passions and desires. Since we live by the Spirit, let us keep in step with the Spirit.

What parts of your life come to mind when you read the words "the flesh with its passions and desires"? Are there any habits or behaviors you could turn over to Christ so that you can "keep in step with the Spirit"?

READ PSALM 51:10

Create in me a pure heart, O God, and renew a steadfast spirit within me.

Remember that, as we heard in the teaching this week, the Holy Spirit can reverse the effects of the Fall and our resulting sinfulness. While we often try to just blend in to any environment in which we find ourselves, God seeks to help us become completely new in Him—and, therefore, distinctly different from the rest of culture.
Offer your heart to Christ; ask to be filled with the Spirit this week.

extra notes

....
....
....
....
....
....
....
....
....
....
....
....
....
....
....
....
....
....

DAILY

DEVOTIONS

As you've done in previous weeks, read each day's Daily Devotion in *The Spirit-Filled Life* companion book. We hope that this devotional time is becoming a regular part of your daily routine. God promises to be present with us as we take time to pray and study His Word. This week, why not pray before your devotional time and ask God to lead you and guide your thoughts as you reflect on the teaching?

EQUIPPED

The Gifts of the Spirit

And now these three remain: faith, hope and love. But the greatest of these is love.

1 CORINTHIANS 13:13

Last week, we learned that all Christians should manifest all of the fruit of the Spirit. This week, however, in our exploration of the gifts of the Holy Spirit, we learn that each of us in the Body of Christ has unique gifts and roles to play.

Christ alone was the person who displayed every gift of the Holy Spirit. He healed others, prophesied, and worked miracles. He was a wise and knowledgeable teacher. As Christians—or "little Christs"—we each serve different purposes within the church and in the world around us. And whenever we exercise the gift we've been given, we bring glory to God.

THIS WEEK, BE PREPARED TO ASK QUESTIONS SUCH AS:

- How do I identify my spiritual gift?
- Are some spiritual gifts more important than others?
- What am I doing to put my spiritual gifts into practice? What else can I do?

SHARE *your* STORY

Open your group with prayer. This should be a brief, simple prayer in which you invite God to guide you and give you insight as you meet. You can pray for specific requests at the end of the meeting, or stop momentarily to pray if a particular situation comes up during your discussion.

If you prefer, you could use this collect from the *Book of Common Prayer* (BCP, p. 70):

O God, who dost manifest in thy servants the signs of thy presence: Send forth upon us the Spirit of love, that in companionship with one another thine abounding grace may increase among us; through Jesus Christ our Lord. Amen.

Telling our personal stories builds deeper connections among group members. Begin your time together by using the following questions and activities to get people talking.

1. What spiritual gifts seem to be most highly regarded within the church? Preaching? Healing prayer? Teaching?

2. What spiritual gift or gifts has God given you? When have you put that gift—or those gifts—to use? What was the result?

extra NOTES

WATCH *now*

DVD SESSION FOUR

_____

_____

_____

_____

_____

_____

_____

_____

_____

_____

_____

_____

_____

_____

Watch the DVD for this session now. Use the Notes space to record your thoughts, questions, and ponderings as you watch the video and discuss the Bible passage.

HEAR *God's* STORY

READ 1 CORINTHIANS 13:1-3

Use the following questions to guide your discussion of the Bible passage and the teaching and stories you just experienced on the DVD.

If I speak in the tongues of men or of angels, but do not have love, I am only a resounding gong or a clanging cymbal. If I have the gift of prophecy and can fathom all mysteries and all knowledge, and if I have a faith that can move mountains, but do not have love, I am nothing. If I give all I possess to the poor and give over my body to hardship that I may boast, but do not have love, I gain nothing.

1. Read this passage again and listen for the sounds it includes. What do you hear? A gong? Flowery speech? Crashing, discordant cymbals? Why do you think the author, St. Paul, chose to include those particular auditory images to represent a lack of love?

2. What can you learn about God's priorities and heart in these verses?

extra notes

NOTES

WE NEED EACH OTHER. Fr. Charlie noted that St. Paul, in his letter to the Corinthians, was compelled to drive the point home that *all* of the gifts of the Holy Spirit are important; it isn't "better" to speak in tongues than to have faith, for instance— even if speaking in tongues might be seen as a "showier" gift to have.

USE YOUR GIFTS. We discern our unique gifts through putting into practice and exercising the gifts. We all have God-given spiritual gifts and, like the parts of the human body, we must work together for our mutual health and purpose.

CREATE *a* NEW STORY

God wants you to be a part of His Kingdom— to weave your story into His. That will mean change—to go His way rather than your own. This won't happen overnight, but it should happen steadily. By starting with small, simple choices, we begin to change our direction. The Holy Spirit helps us along the way: giving us gifts to serve the body, offering us insights into Scripture, and challenging us to love not only those around us but also those far from God.

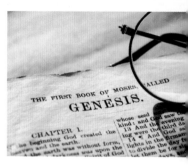

In this section, talk about how you will apply the wisdom you've learned in this session.

1. This week, did you brainstorm about what your own spiritual gifts might be? Describe your thinking.

2. Think of a time when you were able to handle a crisis or conflict and employed gifts you didn't know you had. In what ways did you surprise yourself? In what ways were you stronger or braver than you expected you'd be?

3. Think about your small group or broader church community as the Body of Christ. What roles are sometimes overlooked? What gifts are more highly prized than others?

4. Each of you in the group has different spiritual gifts. And every small group has tasks and roles that need to be completed and filled. How could you serve this group—perhaps with hospitality, prayer, organizing an event, researching or studying a topic, leading worship, or inviting new people? Have each person share what their gift or passion is and how they could use it to strengthen and build up the group.

5. Spend some time praying about those you know who might respond to a simple invitation: to come to a church service, to join your small group, or even to just have coffee and talk about spiritual matters. Ask the Holy Spirit to bring to mind people you can pray for.

6. Groups grow closer when they serve together. How could you as a group serve someone in need? You may want to visit a shut-in from your church, provide a meal for a family going through difficulty, or give some other practical help to someone in need. If nothing comes to mind, spend some time as a group praying and asking God to show you who needs your help. Have two or three group members organize a service project for the group, and then—do it!

for ADDITIONAL STUDY

Take some time between now and our next meeting to dig into God's Word. Explore the Bible passages related to this session's theme on your own, jotting your reflections in a journal or in this study guide. You may even want to use a Bible website or app to look up commentary on these passages. If you like, share what you learn with the group the next time you meet.

READ HEBREWS 2:3-4

This salvation, which was first announced by the Lord, was confirmed to us by those who heard him. God also testified to it by signs, wonders and various miracles, and by gifts of the Holy Spirit distributed according to his will.

God "distributes" spiritual gifts, but how do you know what yours might be? In his teaching this week, Fr. Charlie encourages us to "eagerly desire" to know what our gifts are and ask God to show us. He said we must *use* our talents and gifts, *listen* to the way others describe our skills or areas in which we excel, and *pay attention* to where God seems to be placing and using us. Do you feel confident about your spiritual gifts? If not, how can you better discern what they are?

READ 1 CORINTHIANS 12:4-7

There are different kinds of gifts, but the same Spirit distributes them. There are different kinds of service, but the same Lord. There are different kinds of working, but in all of them and in everyone it is the same God at work. Now to each one the manifestation of the Spirit is given for the common good.

As you look around your small group, what gifts and talents do you discern among the members? Between meeting times, be intentional about affirming one or more members of your group. Tell them how God might have a special purpose in this time and place for their gifts and talents. Think of times you felt most blessed by these individuals. Commit with one another to be unified as a body of believers and to continue to reflect on what it means, corporately, to be a manifestation of Christ's presence and to glorify God with your gifts.

extra notes

....

....

....

....

....

....

....

....

....

....

....

....

....

....

....

....

....

....

....

DAILY

DEVOTIONS

The Daily Devotions for this week, found in *The Spirit-Filled Life* companion book, will further explore these issues. The Daily Devotions are a wonderful way to keep alert to the presence of the Holy Spirit with you throughout the week.

EMPOWERED
The Work of the Spirit

But we have this treasure in jars of clay to show that this all-surpassing power is from God and not from us.

2 CORINTHIANS 4:7

This week, as we further explore *The Spirit-Filled Life*, we examine the difference between living according to the flesh and living in the flesh—concepts the Apostle Paul carefully defined in his writing.

Fr. Charlie cautions us in this week's teaching that when we decide to renounce fleshly desires and live in step with the Holy Spirit, we often find ourselves pushing against spiritual forces that are stronger than we expected.

Part of the Christian call, he reminds us, is to battle against forces of evil in the world. Fortunately, the Holy Spirit is never overcome by the dark powers of the world or by our sinful desires. Battling these things, however, reveals our own weakness and need for Christ.

We are, as St. Paul so aptly describes us, "jars of clay," but the Holy Spirit in us accomplishes God's work despite our fragility. This week we look at how God's strength is revealed in our own weakness.

SHARE *your* STORY

Open your group with prayer. This should be a brief, simple prayer, in which you invite God to give you wisdom and compassion as you meet. You can pray for specific requests at the end of the meeting or stop momentarily to pray if a particular situation comes up during your discussion.

You may wish to use this collect from the *Book of Common Prayer* (BCP, p. 164):

O God, the strength of all who put their trust in thee:
Mercifully accept our prayers; and because through the
weakness of our mortal nature, we can do no good thing
without thee, give us the help of thy grace, that in keeping
thy commandments we may please thee both in will and deed;
through Jesus Christ our Lord, who liveth and reigneth with
thee and the Holy Spirit, one God, for ever and ever. Amen.

Telling our personal stories builds deeper connections among group members. Begin your time together by using the following questions and activities to get people talking. Sharing our stories requires us to be honest. We can help one another to be honest and open by creating a safe place: be sure that your group is one where confidentiality is respected, where there is no such thing as a "stupid question," where you listen without criticizing one another.

1. When is the last time you used the word "evil" or heard someone else use it?

2. Our world is full of conflict, wars, and evil. When you watch the news or see the headlines, what feelings or thoughts do you experience about the state of the world?

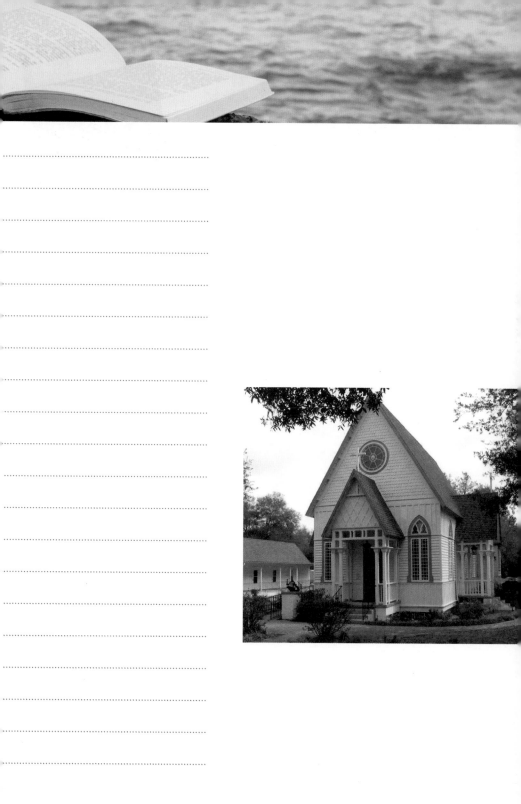

WATCH *now*

DVD SESSION FIVE

Watch the DVD for this session now. Use the Notes space to record your thoughts, questions, and ponderings as you watch the video and discuss the Bible passage.

HEAR *God's* STORY

1. Does reading this verse evoke any emotions in your heart or images in your mind? How do you feel when you talk about these things? Frightened? Confident? Indifferent? Unsure?

   > Be alert and of sober mind. Your enemy the devil prowls around like a roaring lion looking for someone to devour. (1 Peter 5:8)

2. What does it mean to have a "sober mind"? What gets in the way of being alert and sober-minded?

3. Fr. Charlie uses the phrase "the *now*, but *not yet*" to describe the age in which we find ourselves—post-resurrection but prior to the second coming of Christ. In what ways do you feel like your time in spiritual history is an in-between time? When you imagine Christ's coming, how do you picture it?

4. Do you give much attention or notice to the reality that you have a spiritual enemy? What happens when we ignore or underestimate the intentions and purposes of an enemy?

5. How does the discussion of "principalities" and "dark forces" or "the enemy" make you feel?

STUDY

NOTES

OUR THREE ADVERSARIES. Fr. Charlie listed three adversaries Christians must battle as we bring about the Kingdom of Heaven in this life.

They are:

- Satan and the spiritual forces of evil

- Evil powers of the world

- Our sinful desires

Although these forces are formidable, the Holy Spirit in us is stronger than they are. As we share the Good News with others and God's Spirit and presence multiplies, these forces are "unseated" and stripped of their power. God's kingdom is on offense!

CREATE *a* NEW STORY

God wants you to be a part of His Kingdom—to weave your story into His. That will mean change. It will require you to go His way rather than your own. This won't happen overnight, but it should happen steadily. By making small, simple choices, we can begin to change our direction. The Holy Spirit helps us along the way by giving us gifts to serve the body, offering us insights into Scripture, and challenging us to love not only those around us but also those far from God.

In this section, talk about how you will apply the wisdom you've learned in this session.

1. In the Bible verse we read above, we are told to be alert and sober minded. What specific steps can you take to be more alert, spiritually and otherwise?

2. When have you felt aware of a spiritual evil in the world or close by you? Did you draw upon the power of the Holy Spirit in that moment? How would a person practically do that?

3. When do you most feel like a "jar of clay"? How might you turn this weakness over to Christ, trusting in His power, despite your frailty?

4. Spend some time praying about those you know who might respond to a simple invitation: to come to a church service, to join your small group, or even to just have coffee and talk about spiritual matters. Ask the Holy Spirit to bring to mind people you can pray for.

5. A strong group is made up of people who are all being filled up by the Spirit of God, so that they are empowered to love one another. What specific steps will you take this week to connect with God privately, so that He can fill you with all of His fullness in Spirit and Truth? If you've focused on prayer in past weeks, maybe you'll want to add reading and meditating on Scripture this week. If you've been reading God's Word consistently, perhaps you'll want to take it deeper and try memorizing a verse. Tell the group which one you plan to try this week, and then, at your next meeting, talk about your progress and challenges.

6. To close your time together, spend some time worshiping God— praying, singing, reading Scripture.

7. Ask everyone to share: "How can we pray for you this week?" Be sure to write prayer requests on your *Prayer and Praise Report* on page 128.

8. Close your meeting with prayer.

for ADDITIONAL STUDY

Take some time between now and our next meeting to dig into God's Word. Explore the Bible passages related to this session's theme on your own, jotting your reflections in a journal or in this study guide. You may even want to use a Bible website or app to look up commentary on these passages. If you like, share what you learn with the group the next time you meet.

READ 1 CORINTHIANS 1:25

For the foolishness of God is wiser than human wisdom, and the weakness of God is stronger than human strength.

Fr. Charlie recommends that we share our weaknesses and vulnerabilities with each other—and even "boast" about them. In what ways is that a different message from the one we usually receive from a culture that values independence, indifference, and personal power? Consider how you might risk your reputation with members of your small group and brag about your own frailties and the way—despite those frailties—God works through you.

READ HEBREWS 4:15

For we do not have a high priest who is unable to empathize with our weaknesses, but we have one who has been tempted in every way, just as we are—yet he did not sin.

Throughout the Scripture, we are told that God understands—even empathizes—with our weaknesses. When He became incarnate, Jesus Himself came to know what it's like to live in a body that could be wounded, broken, and weary. He, too, came to know what it was like to live in a "jar of clay." In what ways do you see Christ working through you, despite your frailties and weaknesses? What does it tell you about the nature of God that He so often extolled the virtues of those who were meek, who grieved, and who were broken?

extra notes

DAILY

DEVOTIONS

This week, the Daily Devotions in *The Spirit-Filled Life* book explore what it means to be a spirit-filled person in this "now, but not yet" time. Like a multi-faceted diamond, the Daily Devotions uncover the many sides of the text and allow you to experience the light of God's truth from different angles. Be sure to take time each day for these devotional reflections.

ANOINTED

The Mission of the Spirit

The Spirit of the Lord is on me, because he has anointed me to proclaim good news to the poor. He has sent me to proclaim freedom for the prisoners and recovery of sight for the blind, to set the oppressed free.

LUKE 4:18

One of the many names for Jesus is "the anointed one," but to what does that refer? That He was marked with oil? Set apart for a certain mission? Special or honored somehow?

In our last session of *The Spirit-Filled Life*, we consider what it means that we, like Christ, are "anointed."

Fr. Charlie, in his teaching this week, explains that as "little Christs" ourselves, we are "anointed ones" with priestly, prophetic, and kingly responsibilities that echo those that Christ filled during His earthly ministry.

We will consider the unlikely—but wonderful opportunity—to serve in these three roles in our own lives as we more deeply enter the spirit-filled life.

SHARE *your* STORY

Open your group with prayer. This should be a brief, simple prayer in which you invite God to be with you as you meet. You can pray for specific requests at the end of the meeting or stop momentarily to pray if a particular situation comes up during your discussion.

You could also use this prayer from the *Book of Common Prayer*, fitting with the week's theme (BCP, p. 816-817):

Everliving God, whose will it is that all should come to you through your Son Jesus Christ: Inspire our witness to him, that all may know the power of his forgiveness and the hope of his resurrection; who lives and reigns with you and the Holy Spirit, one God, now and for ever. Amen.

As we have said in previous lessons, sharing our personal stories builds deeper connections among group members. Your story may be exactly what another person needs to hear to encourage or strengthen them. And your listening to others' stories is an act of love and kindness to them—and could very well help them to grow spiritually. Begin your time together by using the following questions and activities to get people talking.

1. What has surprised you most about this group? Where did God meet, surprise, or feel most present to you over the last six weeks?

2. What does the word "anointed" mean to you?

3. Take time in this final session to connect in groups of two or three and discuss: What has God been showing you through these sessions about what it means to live in community? Check in with each other about the progress you have made in your spiritual growth during this study.

4. Take some time for each person to share about how they've done with inviting the people on the *Circles of Life* to church or your small group. What specific conversations are you praying about for the weeks to come?

extra NOTES

....

....

....

....

....

....

....

....

....

....

....

....

WATCH *now*

DVD SESSION SIX

Watch the DVD for this session now. Use the Notes space to record your thoughts, questions, and ponderings as you watch the video and discuss the Bible passage.

HEAR *God's* STORY

Use the following questions to guide your discussion of the teaching you just experienced in the video and the Bible passage below.

READ 1 PETER 2:9

But you are a chosen people, a royal priesthood, a holy nation, God's special possession, that you may declare the praises of him who called you out of darkness into his wonderful light.

1. Take a moment—maybe for the first time—to consider what this is saying. You (you!) are chosen, a priest, special to God. When you think of yourself as a "royal priest," what does this mean to you? What are a priest's primary responsibilities?

2. What does it mean to be called out of darkness? What specific darkness did God call you out of?

3. Prophets and kings were—and are—also commonly "anointed" with oil. They are set apart, honored, and consecrated to God. What are some of the roles you play that might also be associated with prophets or kings?

extra notes

STUDY

NOTES

PROPHETS, PRIESTS, AND KINGS.

In the teaching, Fr. Charlie declares that, as believers, we are all anointed ones and we—as Christ did—fill the roles of prophets, priests, and kings.

- We are **prophets** when we proclaim the Good News and coming of Christ to others.

- We are **priests** because we serve as "ambassadors" of God's forgiveness.

- We are **kings** when we fight spiritual battles and work to unseat evil powers.

With which of these three "job descriptions" do you most identify? Which seem(s) out of reach?

CREATE *a* NEW STORY

How has God changed your story during this six-week study? What new things is He asking you to do? What truth has transformed your heart?

Think about specific steps you want to take to live a new story, to walk more closely with God so that you can be a part of His story, engaged in His kingdom.

1. In the teaching, we heard that, in Christ, each of us is uniquely anointed by the filling and indwelling of the Holy Spirit to fulfill God's calling. In what ways does the work you currently engage in align with God's anointing and calling of you?

2. Finish this sentence: "I can better walk in step with the Holy Spirit by _____."

3. In what new ways do you view yourself as anointed by the Spirit of God?

4. How can you and other members of your small group be more mindful of the gifts of the Holy Spirit in each other?

5. What is one way you can declare God's praises in the coming week?

6. As this is the last meeting in this study, take some time to celebrate

the work God has done in the lives of group members. Have each person in the group share some step of growth that they have noticed in *another* member. (In other words, no one will talk about themselves. Instead, affirm others in the group.) Make sure that each person gets affirmed and noticed and celebrated—whether the steps they've made are large or small.

7. If your group still needs to make decisions about continuing to meet after this session, have that discussion now. Talk about what you will study, who will lead, and where and when you will meet.

8. Review your *Small Group Agreement* on page 124 and evaluate how well you met your goals. Discuss any changes you want to make as you move forward. If you plan to continue meeting, and your group starts a new study, this is a great time to take on a new role or change roles of service in your group. What new role will you take on? If you are uncertain, maybe your group members have some ideas for you. Remember you aren't making a lifetime commitment to the new role; it will only be for a few weeks. Maybe someone would like to share a role with you if you don't feel ready to serve solo.

9. Close by praying for your prayer requests and take a couple of minutes to review the praises you have recorded over the past five weeks on the *Prayer and Praise Report* on page 128. Spend some time just worshiping God and thanking Him for all He's done in your group during this study.

DAILY

DEVOTIONS

Continue on your journey through this week's Daily Devotions, found in *The Spirit-Filled Life* companion book. As you do so, ask God to take you deeper into His Word and help you more fully understand the active role of the Holy Spirit in your life.

APPENDICES

FREQUENTLY *asked* QUESTIONS

What do we do on the first night of our group?

Like all fun things in life—have a party! A "get to know you" coffee, dinner, or dessert is a great way to launch a new study. You may want to review the Small Group Agreement (page 124) and share the names of a few friends you can invite to join you. But most importantly, have fun before your study time begins.

Where do we find new members for our group?

We encourage you to pray with your group and then brainstorm a list of people from work, church, your neighborhood, your children's school, family, the gym, and so forth. Then have each group member invite several of the people on his or her list.

No matter how you find participants, it's vital that you stay on the lookout for new people to join your group. All groups tend to go through healthy attrition—the result of moves, releasing new leaders, ministry opportunities, and so forth—and if the group gets too small, it could be at risk of shutting down. If you and your group stay open, you'll be amazed at the people God sends your way. The next person just might become a friend for life. You never know!

How long will this group meet?

It's totally up to the group—once you come to the end of this six-week study. Most groups meet weekly for at least their first six weeks, but every other week can work as well.

At the end of this study, each group member may decide if he or she wants to continue on for another six-week study. Some groups launch relationships for years to come, and others are stepping-stones into another group experience. Either way, enjoy the journey.

What if this group is not working for us?

You're not alone! This could be the result of a personality conflict, life-stage difference, geographical distance, level of spiritual maturity, or any number of things. Relax. Pray for God's direction, and at the end of this six-week study, decide whether to continue with this group or find another. You don't usually buy the first car you look at or marry the first person you date, and the same goes with a group. Don't bail out before the 6 weeks are up—God might have something to teach you. Also, don't run from conflict or prejudge people before you have given them a chance. God is still working in you, too!

How do we handle the childcare needs in our group?

We suggest that you empower the group to openly brainstorm solutions. You may try one option that works for a while and then adjust over time. Our favorite approach is for adults to meet in the living room or dining room and to share the cost of a babysitter (or two) who can be with the kids in a different part of the house. In this way, parents don't have to be away from their children all evening when their children are too young to be left at home. A second option is to use one home for the kids and a second home (close by or a phone call away) for the adults. A third idea is to rotate the responsibility of providing a lesson or care for the children either in the same home or in another home nearby. This can be an incredible blessing for kids. Finally, the most common idea is to decide that you need to have a night to invest in your spiritual lives individually or as a couple and to make your own arrangements for childcare. No matter what decision the group makes, the best approach is to dialogue openly about both the problem and the solution.

SMALL *group* AGREEMENT

OUR PURPOSE:
To talk about what it means to live a God-first life with a few friends.

Group Attendance	To give priority to the group meeting. We will call or email if we will be late or absent. (Completing the Group Calendar on page 126 will minimize this issue.)
Safe Environment	To help create a safe place where people can be heard and feel loved.
Respect Differences	To be gentle and gracious toward different spiritual maturity, personal opinions, temperaments, or "imperfections" in fellow group members. We are all works in progress.
Confidentiality	To keep anything that is shared strictly confidential and within the group, and to avoid sharing improper information about those outside the group.
Encouragement for Growth	Accept one another as we are while encouraging one another to grow.
Shared Ownership	To remember that every member is a minister and to ensure that each attender will share a small team role or responsibility over time.
Rotating Hosts/ Leaders and Homes	To encourage different people to host the group in their homes, and to rotate the responsibility of facilitating each meeting. (See the Group Calendar on page 126).

OUR *time* TOGETHER

Refreshments/mealtimes will be provided by:

The arrangement for childcare will be:

When we will meet (day of week):

Where we will meet (place):

We will begin at (time):

We will do our best to have some or all of us attend a worship service together. Our primary worship service time will be:

Date of this agreement:

Date we will review this agreement again:

SMALL *group* CALENDAR

DATE	LESSON	HOST HOME	REFRESHMENTS	LEADER
Monday Jan 15	1	Bill	Joe	Bill

MEMORY VERSES

1

SESSION ONE: BAPTIZED
And hope does not put us to shame, because God's love has been poured out into our hearts through the Holy Spirit, who has been given to us.
(Romans 5:5)

2

SESSION TWO: ADOPTED
He predestined us for adoption to sonship through Jesus Christ, in accordance with his pleasure and will.
(Ephesians 1:5)

3

SESSION THREE: TRANSFORMED
Do not conform to the pattern of this world, but be transformed by the renewing of your mind. Then you will be able to test and approve what God's will is—his good, pleasing and perfect will.
(Romans 12:2)

4

SESSION FOUR: EQUIPPED
And now these three remain: faith, hope and love. But the greatest of these is love.
(I Corinthians 13:13)

5

SESSION FIVE: EMPOWERED
But we have this treasure in jars of clay to show that this all-surpassing power is from God and not from us.
(2 Corinthians 4:7)

6

SESSION SIX: ANOINTED
The Spirit of the Lord is on me, because he has anointed me to proclaim good news to the poor. He has sent me to proclaim freedom for the prisoners and recovery of sight for the blind, to set the oppressed free.
(Luke 4:18)

PRAYER & PRAISE
REPORT

10.01.15 — Praying on behalf of Brian to strengthen & grow his consistency in is Spiritual ministry within his office.

— Praying on behalf of Nina & her close friend relationships, to foster & strengthen these ties & create more time with them.

10.08.15 — Praying for Mitzy & her health

— Pray for Nina's time, how does God intend to use her time & gifts.

10.29.15 — Praise

11.03.15 — Cont. praise for lengthening the durations of no fever for Brian. Mitzy has returned to work and God has changed her heart through her medical trial of thyroid canc

Prayer for Brian's bloodwork results.
Prayer for Shelby's UC symptoms.
Prayer for safe travels to G-ville
for Nina & me.
Prayers for peace for Nina & work.
Prayers for Brian's retreat at St. Leo.
Prayers for safe travels to Dunnellon
for Nina & peace while there.

11.12.15 - Praises for Brian's
healing & <u>NO</u> elevated temp.
    Prayer for safe travels
to S.C. for George Helm & friends.
    Prayer for Shelby's
treatment of UC over the
weekend.
    Prayers for Nina's health
& intestinal upset.

SMALL *group* ROSTER

	PRAYER REQUESTS	PRAISE REPORTS
SESSION 1		
SESSION 2		
SESSION 3		
SESSION 4		
SESSION 5		
SESSION 6		

HOSTING *an* OPEN HOUSE

If you're starting a new group, or if this is your first time leading a small group, you should consider planning an "open house" before your first formal group meeting. Even if you only have two to four core members, it's a great way to break the ice and to consider prayerfully who else might be open to join you over the next few weeks. You can also use this kick-off meeting to hand out study guides, spend some time getting to know each other, discuss each person's expectations for the group, and briefly pray for each other.

A simple meal or good desserts always make a kick-off meeting more fun. After people introduce themselves and share how they ended up being at the meeting, have everyone respond to a few icebreaker questions, like: "What is your favorite family vacation?" or "What is one thing you love about your church/our community?" or "What are three things about your life growing up that most people here don't know?" Finally, ask everyone to tell what he or she hopes to get out of the study. You might want to review the Small Group Agreement and talk about each person's expectations and priorities.

You can skip this kick-off meeting if your time is limited, but an open house can help set your group up for success.

LEADING *for* THE FIRST TIME

Sweaty palms are a healthy sign.
The Bible says God is gracious to the humble. Remember who is in control. Those who are soft in heart (and sweaty palmed) are those whom God is sure to speak through. God wants to use you exactly as you are to lead your group this week.

Seek support.
Ask your co-leader or a close friend to pray for you and prepare with you before the session. Walking through the study will help you anticipate potentially difficult questions and discussion topics.

Prepare.
Prepare. Prepare. Go through the session several times prior to meeting. If you are using the DVD, watch the teaching segment. Consider writing in a journal or fasting for a day to prepare yourself for what God wants to do.

Ask for feedback so you can grow.
Perhaps in an email or on cards handed out at the study, have everyone write down three things you did well and one thing you could improve. Don't get defensive; instead, show an openness to learn and grow.

Share with your group what God is doing in your heart.
God is searching for those whose hearts are fully His. Share your struggles and your victories. People will relate and your willingness to share will encourage them to do the same.

LEADERSHIP TRAINING *101*

Congratulations! You have responded to the call to help shepherd Jesus' flock. There are few other tasks in the family of God that surpass the contribution you will be making. As you prepare to lead, whether it is one session or the entire series, here are a few thoughts to keep in mind. We encourage you to read these and review them with each new discussion leader before he or she leads.

1. **Remember that you are not alone.** God knows everything about you, and He knew that you would be asked to lead your group. Remember that it is common for all good leaders to feel that they are not ready to lead. Moses, Solomon, Jeremiah, and Timothy were all reluctant to lead. God promises, "Never will I leave you; never will I forsake you" (Hebrews 13:5). Whether you are leading for one evening, for several weeks, or for a lifetime, you will be blessed as you serve.

2. **Don't try to do it alone.** Pray right now for God to help you build a healthy leadership team. If you can enlist a co-leader to help you lead the group, you will find your experience to be much richer. This is your chance to involve as many people as you can in building a healthy group. All you have to do is call and ask people to help. You'll probably be surprised at the response.

3. **Just be yourself.** If you won't be you, who will? God wants you to use your unique gifts and temperament. Don't try to do things exactly like another leader; do them in a way that fits you! Just admit it when you don't have an answer, and apologize when you make a mistake. Your group will love you for it, and you'll sleep better at night!

4. **Prepare for your meeting ahead of time.** Review the session and the leader's notes, and write down your responses to each question. Pay special attention to exercises that ask group members to do something other than engage in discussion. These exercises will help your group live what the Bible teaches, not just talk about it. Be sure you understand how an exercise works, and bring any necessary supplies (such as paper and pens) to your meeting. If the exercise employs one of the items in the appendix, be sure to look over that item so you'll know how it works. Finally, review "Outline for Each Session" so you'll remember the purpose of each section in the study.

5. **Pray for your group members by name.** Before you begin your session, go around the room in your mind and pray for each member by name. You may want to review the prayer list at least once a week. Ask God to use your time together to touch the heart of every person uniquely. Expect God to lead you to whomever He wants you to encourage or challenge in a special way. If you listen, God will surely lead!

6. When you ask a question, be patient. Someone will eventually respond. Sometimes people need a moment or two of silence to think about the question. Keep in mind, if silence doesn't bother you, it won't bother anyone else. After someone responds, affirm the response with a simple "thanks" or "good job." Then ask, "How about somebody else?" or "Would someone who hasn't shared like to add anything?" Be sensitive to new people or reluctant members who aren't ready to say, pray, or do anything. If you give them a safe setting, they will blossom over time.

7. Provide transitions between questions. When guiding the discussion, always read aloud the transitional paragraphs and the questions. Ask the group if anyone would like to read the paragraph or Bible passage. Don't call on anyone, but ask for a volunteer, and then be patient until someone begins. Be sure to thank the person who reads aloud.

8. Break up into small groups each week or they won't stay. If your group has more than seven people, we strongly encourage you to have the group gather sometimes in discussion circles of three or four people during the *Hear God's Story* or *Change Your Story* sections of the study. With a greater opportunity to talk in a small circle, people will connect more with the study, apply more quickly what they're learning and ultimately get more out of it. A small circle also encourages a quiet person to participate and tends to minimize the effects of a more vocal or dominant member. It can also help people feel more loved in your group. When you gather again at the end of the section, you can have one person summarize the highlights from each circle. Small circles are also helpful during prayer time. People who are unaccustomed to praying aloud will feel more comfortable trying it with just two or three others. Also, prayer requests won't take as much time, so circles will have more time to actually pray. When you gather back with the whole group, you can have one person from each circle briefly update everyone on the prayer requests. People are more willing to pray in small circles if they know that the whole group will hear all the prayer requests.

9. Rotate facilitators weekly. At the end of each meeting, ask the group who should lead the following week. Let the group help select your weekly facilitator. You may be perfectly capable of leading each time, but you will help others grow in their faith and gifts if you give them opportunities to lead. You can use the Small Group Calendar to fill in the names of all meeting leaders at once if you prefer.

10. One final challenge (for new or first-time leaders):
Before your first opportunity to lead, look up each of the five passages listed below. Read each one as a devotional exercise to help equip yourself with a shepherd's heart. Trust us on this one. If you do this, you will be more than ready for your first meeting.

Matthew 9:36
1 Peter 5:2-4
Psalm 23
Ezekiel 34:11-16
1 Thessalonians 2:7-8, 11-12

NOTES

NOTES

Artwork Attribution

Page 19 The Pentecost (oil on canvas), Galloche, Louis (1670-1761) / Musee des Beaux-Arts, Nantes, France / Bridgeman Images

Page 30 The Baptism of Christ, c.1597 (oil on canvas), Greco, El (Domenico Theotocopuli) (1541-1614) / Prado, Madrid, Spain / Peter Willi / Bridgeman Images

Page 46 Vision of St. John of Matha, by Giovanni Antonio Guardi, 18th Century, canvas, Guardi, Giovanni Antonio (1698-1760) / Mondadori Portfolio/Electa/Elio Ciol / Bridgeman Images

Page 51 Ms Lat. Q.v.I.126 f.90 The Holy Spirit, from the 'Book of Hours of Louis d'Orleans', 1469 (vellum), Colombe, Jean (c.1430-c.93) / National Library, St. Petersburg, Russia / Bridgeman Images

Page 64 The Transfiguration, 1594-95 (oil on canvas), Carracci, Lodovico (1555-1619) / Pinacoteca Nazionale, Bologna, Italy / Bridgeman Images

Page 82 St. Francis Xavier Blessing the Sick (oil on canvas), Rubens, Peter Paul (1577-1640) / Kunsthistorisches Museum, Vienna, Austria / Bridgeman Images

Page 97 Archangel Michael Defeating Satan, c.1636 (oil on canvas), Reni, Guido (1575-1642) / Santa Maria della Concezione, Rome, Italy / Bridgeman Images

Page 98 The Heavenly Militia, c.1348-54 (tempera on panel), Guariento, Ridolfo di Arpo (c.1310-c.1370) / Museo Civico, Padua, Italy / Bridgeman Images

Page 115 The Entry of Christ into Jerusalem (oil on panel), Santi di Tito (1536-1603) / Galleria dell' Accademia, Florence, Italy / Bridgeman Images